# 50 Premium Hamburger Recipes

By: Kelly Johnson

# Table of Contents

- Classic Cheeseburger
- BBQ Bacon Burger
- Mushroom Swiss Burger
- Jalapeño Popper Burger
- Mediterranean Lamb Burger
- Teriyaki Pineapple Burger
- Blue Cheese Burger
- Chipotle Black Bean Burger
- Garlic Aioli Turkey Burger
- Korean BBQ Burger
- Avocado Bacon Burger
- Spicy Sriracha Burger
- Greek Feta Burger
- Smoky BBQ Pulled Pork Burger
- Southwest Chipotle Burger
- Caprese Burger with Basil Pesto
- Sliders with Dill Pickle Relish
- Thai Peanut Chicken Burger
- Sweet and Spicy Mango Burger
- Italian Meatball Burger
- Breakfast Burger with Fried Egg
- Vegan Quinoa Burger
- Balsamic Glazed Burger
- Tex-Mex Burger with Guacamole
- Buffalo Chicken Burger
- Thai Basil Chicken Burger
- Roasted Red Pepper and Feta Burger
- Pesto Mozzarella Burger
- Cajun-Spiced Burger
- Blackened Salmon Burger
- Lobster and Avocado Burger
- Fig and Goat Cheese Burger
- Reuben Burger with Sauerkraut
- Bacon Cheddar Ranch Burger
- Spicy Mediterranean Turkey Burger

- Chipotle Turkey Burger with Avocado
- Maple Glazed Burger with Bacon
- Pimento Cheese Burger
- BBQ Brisket Burger
- Cucumber Dill Burger
- Sweet Potato Black Bean Burger
- Huli Huli Chicken Burger
- Bourbon BBQ Burger
- Garlic Parmesan Burger
- Curry Chickpea Burger
- Apple and Gouda Burger
- Dill Pickle Chicken Burger
- Steakhouse Burger with Caramelized Onions
- Lobster Roll Burger
- Fig and Bacon Burger

**Classic Cheeseburger**

**Ingredients:**

- 1 lb ground beef (80/20)
- Salt and pepper to taste
- 4 slices cheddar cheese
- 4 hamburger buns
- Lettuce, tomato, and onion for toppings
- Ketchup and mustard for serving

**Instructions:**

1. **Preheat Grill**: Preheat your grill or stovetop skillet over medium-high heat.
2. **Form Patties**: Divide the ground beef into four equal portions and shape them into patties. Season both sides with salt and pepper.
3. **Cook Patties**: Grill the patties for about 4-5 minutes on one side. Flip and cook for an additional 3-4 minutes.
4. **Add Cheese**: During the last minute of cooking, place a slice of cheddar cheese on each patty and cover until melted.
5. **Assemble**: Toast the buns if desired. Place the burger patties on the bottom half of the buns and top with lettuce, tomato, onion, ketchup, and mustard. Serve immediately.

## BBQ Bacon Burger

**Ingredients:**

- 1 lb ground beef
- Salt and pepper to taste
- 4 slices cheddar cheese
- 4 slices cooked bacon
- 1/2 cup BBQ sauce
- 4 hamburger buns

**Instructions:**

1. **Preheat Grill**: Heat grill to medium-high.
2. **Form Patties**: Shape ground beef into four patties and season with salt and pepper.
3. **Cook Patties**: Grill for 4-5 minutes on one side, then flip and cook for another 3 minutes.
4. **Add Cheese**: Top each patty with cheddar cheese and a slice of bacon. Brush BBQ sauce over the patties and cover until cheese melts.
5. **Assemble**: Place patties on buns and drizzle with extra BBQ sauce. Serve hot.

## Mushroom Swiss Burger

**Ingredients:**

- 1 lb ground beef
- Salt and pepper to taste
- 4 slices Swiss cheese
- 1 cup mushrooms, sliced
- 1 tablespoon olive oil
- 4 hamburger buns

**Instructions:**

1. **Sauté Mushrooms**: In a skillet, heat olive oil over medium heat. Add mushrooms and cook until browned. Season with salt and pepper.
2. **Preheat Grill**: Preheat the grill to medium-high heat.
3. **Form Patties**: Shape ground beef into four patties and season.
4. **Cook Patties**: Grill for about 4-5 minutes on each side, or until cooked to your liking.
5. **Add Cheese and Serve**: During the last minute of cooking, place a slice of Swiss cheese on each patty. Top with sautéed mushrooms and serve on toasted buns.

## Jalapeño Popper Burger

**Ingredients:**

- 1 lb ground beef
- Salt and pepper to taste
- 4 oz cream cheese, softened
- 1/2 cup jalapeños, diced (fresh or pickled)
- 4 slices pepper jack cheese
- 4 hamburger buns

**Instructions:**

1. **Preheat Grill**: Heat grill to medium-high.
2. **Make Filling**: In a bowl, mix cream cheese and jalapeños.
3. **Form Patties**: Shape ground beef into four patties and create a small indent in the center. Fill with jalapeño cream cheese mixture and seal.
4. **Cook Patties**: Grill for about 5-6 minutes on each side until cooked through.
5. **Add Cheese**: Place pepper jack cheese on patties during the last minute. Serve on buns.

## Mediterranean Lamb Burger

**Ingredients:**

- 1 lb ground lamb
- 2 cloves garlic, minced
- 1 tablespoon fresh mint, chopped
- 1 tablespoon fresh parsley, chopped
- Salt and pepper to taste
- 4 pita bread or hamburger buns
- Tzatziki sauce for serving

**Instructions:**

1. **Preheat Grill**: Heat grill to medium-high.
2. **Mix Ingredients**: In a bowl, combine ground lamb, garlic, mint, parsley, salt, and pepper.
3. **Form Patties**: Shape into four patties.
4. **Cook Patties**: Grill for about 5-6 minutes on each side until desired doneness.
5. **Serve**: Serve in pita bread or buns with tzatziki sauce.

## Teriyaki Pineapple Burger

**Ingredients:**

- 1 lb ground beef or chicken
- Salt and pepper to taste
- 4 slices grilled pineapple
- 1/4 cup teriyaki sauce
- 4 hamburger buns
- Lettuce for garnish

**Instructions:**

1. **Preheat Grill**: Heat grill to medium-high.
2. **Form Patties**: Shape meat into four patties and season.
3. **Cook Patties**: Grill for 4-5 minutes per side, basting with teriyaki sauce.
4. **Add Pineapple**: Top each patty with a slice of grilled pineapple during the last minute.
5. **Assemble**: Serve on buns with lettuce and extra teriyaki sauce.

**Blue Cheese Burger**

**Ingredients:**

- 1 lb ground beef
- Salt and pepper to taste
- 4 oz blue cheese, crumbled
- 4 hamburger buns
- Arugula or spinach for garnish

**Instructions:**

1. **Preheat Grill**: Heat grill to medium-high.
2. **Form Patties**: Shape ground beef into four patties and season with salt and pepper.
3. **Cook Patties**: Grill for 4-5 minutes on each side until desired doneness.
4. **Add Blue Cheese**: Top each patty with blue cheese during the last minute.
5. **Serve**: Serve on buns with arugula or spinach.

## Chipotle Black Bean Burger

**Ingredients:**

- 1 can (15 oz) black beans, drained and rinsed
- 1/2 cup breadcrumbs
- 1/4 cup red onion, diced
- 1 tablespoon chipotle sauce
- 1 teaspoon cumin
- Salt and pepper to taste
- 4 hamburger buns

**Instructions:**

1. **Prepare Mixture**: In a bowl, mash black beans and combine with breadcrumbs, onion, chipotle sauce, cumin, salt, and pepper.
2. **Form Patties**: Shape mixture into four patties.
3. **Preheat Grill**: Heat grill to medium-high.
4. **Cook Patties**: Grill for about 5-6 minutes on each side until heated through.
5. **Serve**: Serve on buns with your favorite toppings.

## Garlic Aioli Turkey Burger

**Ingredients:**

- 1 lb ground turkey
- 1/4 cup breadcrumbs
- 2 cloves garlic, minced
- 1 tablespoon Worcestershire sauce
- Salt and pepper to taste
- 4 hamburger buns
- **For Garlic Aioli**:
    - 1/2 cup mayonnaise
    - 1 clove garlic, minced
    - Juice of 1/2 lemon
    - Salt to taste

**Instructions:**

1. **Make Aioli**: In a bowl, mix mayonnaise, minced garlic, lemon juice, and salt. Refrigerate until ready to use.
2. **Preheat Grill**: Heat grill to medium-high.
3. **Mix Turkey**: In a large bowl, combine ground turkey, breadcrumbs, minced garlic, Worcestershire sauce, salt, and pepper. Form into four patties.
4. **Cook Patties**: Grill turkey patties for about 5-6 minutes on each side until cooked through (internal temperature of 165°F/75°C).
5. **Assemble**: Serve turkey burgers on buns with garlic aioli and your favorite toppings.

**Korean BBQ Burger**

**Ingredients:**

- 1 lb ground beef
- 1/4 cup Korean BBQ sauce
- 1 tablespoon soy sauce
- 1 tablespoon sesame oil
- 4 hamburger buns
- Kimchi and green onions for topping

**Instructions:**

1. **Mix Ingredients**: In a bowl, combine ground beef, Korean BBQ sauce, soy sauce, and sesame oil. Form into four patties.
2. **Preheat Grill**: Heat grill to medium-high.
3. **Cook Patties**: Grill for about 4-5 minutes on each side until desired doneness.
4. **Serve**: Serve on buns topped with kimchi and chopped green onions.

**Avocado Bacon Burger**

**Ingredients:**

- 1 lb ground beef or turkey
- Salt and pepper to taste
- 4 slices bacon, cooked
- 1 avocado, sliced
- 4 hamburger buns
- Lettuce and tomato for toppings

**Instructions:**

1. **Preheat Grill**: Heat grill to medium-high.
2. **Form Patties**: Shape ground beef or turkey into four patties and season with salt and pepper.
3. **Cook Patties**: Grill for about 4-5 minutes on each side until cooked through.
4. **Assemble**: Serve on buns topped with bacon, avocado, lettuce, and tomato.

## Spicy Sriracha Burger

**Ingredients:**

- 1 lb ground beef
- 2 tablespoons Sriracha sauce
- 1 tablespoon soy sauce
- Salt and pepper to taste
- 4 hamburger buns
- Jalapeños and spicy mayo for topping

**Instructions:**

1. **Mix Ingredients**: In a bowl, combine ground beef, Sriracha, soy sauce, salt, and pepper. Form into four patties.
2. **Preheat Grill**: Heat grill to medium-high.
3. **Cook Patties**: Grill for about 4-5 minutes on each side until desired doneness.
4. **Serve**: Serve on buns topped with jalapeños and spicy mayo.

**Greek Feta Burger**

**Ingredients:**

- 1 lb ground beef or lamb
- 1/2 cup feta cheese, crumbled
- 1 tablespoon dried oregano
- Salt and pepper to taste
- 4 hamburger buns
- Tzatziki sauce for serving

**Instructions:**

1. **Mix Ingredients**: In a bowl, combine ground meat, feta, oregano, salt, and pepper. Form into four patties.
2. **Preheat Grill**: Heat grill to medium-high.
3. **Cook Patties**: Grill for about 5-6 minutes on each side until cooked through.
4. **Serve**: Serve on buns with tzatziki sauce.

## Smoky BBQ Pulled Pork Burger

**Ingredients:**

- 2 cups pulled pork (cooked)
- 1/2 cup BBQ sauce
- 4 hamburger buns
- Coleslaw for topping

**Instructions:**

1. **Heat Pulled Pork**: In a saucepan, mix pulled pork with BBQ sauce and heat over low heat until warmed through.
2. **Preheat Grill**: Heat grill to medium-high.
3. **Toast Buns**: Lightly toast buns on the grill.
4. **Assemble**: Serve pulled pork on buns topped with coleslaw.

**Southwest Chipotle Burger**

**Ingredients:**

- 1 lb ground beef
- 1 tablespoon chipotle sauce
- 1 teaspoon cumin
- Salt and pepper to taste
- 4 hamburger buns
- Avocado and salsa for topping

**Instructions:**

1. **Mix Ingredients**: In a bowl, combine ground beef, chipotle sauce, cumin, salt, and pepper. Form into four patties.
2. **Preheat Grill**: Heat grill to medium-high.
3. **Cook Patties**: Grill for about 5-6 minutes on each side until cooked through.
4. **Serve**: Serve on buns topped with avocado and salsa.

**Caprese Burger with Basil Pesto**

**Ingredients:**

- 1 lb ground beef
- Salt and pepper to taste
- 4 slices fresh mozzarella cheese
- Fresh basil leaves
- 4 hamburger buns
- 1/4 cup basil pesto

**Instructions:**

1. **Preheat Grill**: Heat grill to medium-high.
2. **Form Patties**: Shape ground beef into four patties and season with salt and pepper.
3. **Cook Patties**: Grill for about 4-5 minutes on one side, flip, and add mozzarella. Cook until melted.
4. **Assemble**: Serve on buns with pesto and fresh basil leaves.

**Sliders with Dill Pickle Relish**

**Ingredients:**

- 1 lb ground beef
- Salt and pepper to taste
- 12 slider buns
- Dill pickle relish for serving

**Instructions:**

1. **Preheat Grill**: Heat grill to medium-high.
2. **Form Sliders**: Shape ground beef into 12 small patties and season.
3. **Cook Sliders**: Grill for about 3-4 minutes on each side until cooked through.
4. **Serve**: Serve on slider buns topped with dill pickle relish.

## Thai Peanut Chicken Burger

**Ingredients:**

- 1 lb ground chicken
- 1/4 cup peanut butter
- 2 tablespoons soy sauce
- 1 tablespoon grated ginger
- 4 hamburger buns
- Sliced cucumbers and cilantro for topping

**Instructions:**

1. **Mix Ingredients**: In a bowl, combine ground chicken, peanut butter, soy sauce, and ginger. Form into four patties.
2. **Preheat Grill**: Heat grill to medium-high.
3. **Cook Patties**: Grill for about 5-6 minutes on each side until cooked through (internal temperature of 165°F/75°C).
4. **Serve**: Serve on buns topped with sliced cucumbers and cilantro.

**Sweet and Spicy Mango Burger**

**Ingredients:**

- 1 lb ground beef or chicken
- 1/2 cup mango salsa
- 1 tablespoon sriracha (adjust to taste)
- 4 hamburger buns
- Lettuce for topping

**Instructions:**

1. **Mix Ingredients**: In a bowl, combine ground meat, mango salsa, and sriracha. Form into four patties.
2. **Preheat Grill**: Heat grill to medium-high.
3. **Cook Patties**: Grill for about 4-5 minutes on each side until desired doneness.
4. **Serve**: Serve on buns with lettuce.

**Italian Meatball Burger**

**Ingredients:**

- 1 lb ground beef
- 1/2 cup breadcrumbs
- 1/4 cup grated Parmesan cheese
- 1 tablespoon Italian seasoning
- 4 hamburger buns
- Marinara sauce and mozzarella cheese for topping

**Instructions:**

1. **Mix Ingredients**: In a bowl, combine ground beef, breadcrumbs, Parmesan, and Italian seasoning. Form into four patties.
2. **Preheat Grill**: Heat grill to medium-high.
3. **Cook Patties**: Grill for about 5-6 minutes on each side until cooked through.
4. **Serve**: Serve on buns topped with marinara sauce and mozzarella cheese.

**Breakfast Burger with Fried Egg**

**Ingredients:**

- 1 lb ground beef or turkey
- Salt and pepper to taste
- 4 slices cheddar cheese
- 4 fried eggs
- 4 hamburger buns
- Bacon or sausage for optional topping

**Instructions:**

1. **Preheat Grill**: Heat grill to medium-high.
2. **Form Patties**: Shape ground meat into four patties and season with salt and pepper.
3. **Cook Patties**: Grill for about 4-5 minutes on each side until desired doneness, adding cheese during the last minute to melt.
4. **Serve**: Assemble with a fried egg on top and any additional toppings desired.

**Vegan Quinoa Burger**

Ingredients:

- 1 cup cooked quinoa
- 1/2 cup black beans, mashed
- 1/4 cup breadcrumbs
- 1 teaspoon cumin
- Salt and pepper to taste
- 4 whole-grain buns
- Avocado and lettuce for topping

Instructions:

1. **Mix Ingredients**: In a bowl, combine cooked quinoa, mashed black beans, breadcrumbs, cumin, salt, and pepper. Form into four patties.
2. **Preheat Grill**: Heat grill to medium-high.
3. **Cook Patties**: Grill for about 4-5 minutes on each side until golden brown.
4. **Serve**: Serve on buns topped with avocado and lettuce.

## Balsamic Glazed Burger

**Ingredients:**

- 1 lb ground beef
- 1/4 cup balsamic vinegar
- 2 tablespoons brown sugar
- Salt and pepper to taste
- 4 hamburger buns
- Arugula or spinach for topping

**Instructions:**

1. **Preheat Grill**: Heat grill to medium-high.
2. **Form Patties**: Shape ground beef into four patties and season with salt and pepper.
3. **Cook Patties**: Grill for about 4-5 minutes on each side. Brush with balsamic mixture (balsamic vinegar and brown sugar) during the last few minutes of cooking.
4. **Serve**: Serve on buns topped with arugula or spinach.

**Tex-Mex Burger with Guacamole**

**Ingredients:**

- 1 lb ground beef or turkey
- 1 tablespoon taco seasoning
- 4 hamburger buns
- Guacamole and salsa for topping
- Pepper jack cheese (optional)

**Instructions:**

1. **Mix Ingredients**: In a bowl, combine ground meat and taco seasoning. Form into four patties.
2. **Preheat Grill**: Heat grill to medium-high.
3. **Cook Patties**: Grill for about 4-5 minutes on each side until desired doneness, adding cheese during the last minute if desired.
4. **Serve**: Serve on buns topped with guacamole and salsa.

**Buffalo Chicken Burger**

**Ingredients:**

- 1 lb ground chicken
- 1/4 cup buffalo sauce
- Salt and pepper to taste
- 4 hamburger buns
- Blue cheese dressing and lettuce for topping

**Instructions:**

1. **Mix Ingredients**: In a bowl, combine ground chicken, buffalo sauce, salt, and pepper. Form into four patties.
2. **Preheat Grill**: Heat grill to medium-high.
3. **Cook Patties**: Grill for about 5-6 minutes on each side until cooked through.
4. **Serve**: Serve on buns topped with blue cheese dressing and lettuce.

**Thai Basil Chicken Burger**

**Ingredients:**

- 1 lb ground chicken
- 1/4 cup Thai basil, chopped
- 1 tablespoon fish sauce
- 1 tablespoon soy sauce
- 4 hamburger buns
- Sliced cucumbers and cilantro for topping

**Instructions:**

1. **Mix Ingredients**: In a bowl, combine ground chicken, chopped Thai basil, fish sauce, and soy sauce. Form into four patties.
2. **Preheat Grill**: Heat grill to medium-high.
3. **Cook Patties**: Grill for about 5-6 minutes on each side until cooked through.
4. **Serve**: Serve on buns topped with sliced cucumbers and cilantro.

## Roasted Red Pepper and Feta Burger

**Ingredients:**

- 1 lb ground beef or turkey
- 1/2 cup roasted red peppers, chopped
- 1/4 cup feta cheese, crumbled
- 1 teaspoon garlic powder
- 4 hamburger buns
- Spinach or arugula for topping

**Instructions:**

1. **Mix Ingredients**: In a bowl, combine ground meat, roasted red peppers, feta cheese, and garlic powder. Form into four patties.
2. **Preheat Grill**: Heat grill to medium-high.
3. **Cook Patties**: Grill for about 4-5 minutes on each side until desired doneness.
4. **Serve**: Serve on buns topped with spinach or arugula.

## Pesto Mozzarella Burger

**Ingredients:**

- 1 lb ground beef or chicken
- 1/4 cup pesto sauce
- 4 slices fresh mozzarella cheese
- 4 hamburger buns
- Fresh basil leaves for topping

**Instructions:**

1. **Mix Ingredients**: In a bowl, combine ground meat and pesto sauce. Form into four patties.
2. **Preheat Grill**: Heat grill to medium-high.
3. **Cook Patties**: Grill for about 4-5 minutes on each side. Add mozzarella slices during the last minute to melt.
4. **Serve**: Serve on buns topped with fresh basil leaves.

**Cajun-Spiced Burger**

**Ingredients:**

- 1 lb ground beef or turkey
- 1 tablespoon Cajun seasoning
- Salt and pepper to taste
- 4 hamburger buns
- Remoulade sauce or mayo for topping

**Instructions:**

1. **Mix Ingredients**: In a bowl, combine ground meat, Cajun seasoning, salt, and pepper. Form into four patties.
2. **Preheat Grill**: Heat grill to medium-high.
3. **Cook Patties**: Grill for about 4-5 minutes on each side until desired doneness.
4. **Serve**: Serve on buns with remoulade sauce or mayo.

## Blackened Salmon Burger

**Ingredients:**

- 1 lb salmon fillet, skin removed
- 1 tablespoon blackening seasoning
- 4 hamburger buns
- Lemon aioli for topping
- Lettuce and tomato for serving

**Instructions:**

1. **Preheat Grill**: Heat grill to medium-high.
2. **Prepare Salmon**: Cut salmon into four equal portions and coat with blackening seasoning.
3. **Cook Salmon**: Grill for about 4-5 minutes on each side until cooked through.
4. **Serve**: Serve on buns with lemon aioli, lettuce, and tomato.

## Lobster and Avocado Burger

**Ingredients:**

- 1 lb cooked lobster meat, chopped
- 1 ripe avocado, mashed
- 1 tablespoon lime juice
- 4 hamburger buns
- Lettuce for topping

**Instructions:**

1. **Mix Ingredients**: In a bowl, combine lobster meat, mashed avocado, and lime juice.
2. **Preheat Grill**: Heat grill to medium-high.
3. **Heat Mixture**: Optionally, grill the lobster mixture briefly to warm it up, about 2 minutes.
4. **Serve**: Serve on buns topped with lettuce.

## Fig and Goat Cheese Burger

**Ingredients:**

- 1 lb ground beef or turkey
- 1/2 cup figs, chopped
- 1/4 cup goat cheese, crumbled
- 4 hamburger buns
- Arugula or mixed greens for topping

**Instructions:**

1. **Mix Ingredients**: In a bowl, combine ground meat, chopped figs, and goat cheese. Form into four patties.
2. **Preheat Grill**: Heat grill to medium-high.
3. **Cook Patties**: Grill for about 4-5 minutes on each side until desired doneness.
4. **Serve**: Serve on buns topped with arugula or mixed greens.

**Reuben Burger with Sauerkraut**

**Ingredients:**

- 1 lb ground beef
- 1 teaspoon caraway seeds
- 4 slices Swiss cheese
- 1 cup sauerkraut, drained
- 4 hamburger buns
- Thousand Island dressing for topping

**Instructions:**

1. **Mix Ingredients**: In a bowl, combine ground beef and caraway seeds. Form into four patties.
2. **Preheat Grill**: Heat grill to medium-high.
3. **Cook Patties**: Grill for about 4-5 minutes on each side. Add Swiss cheese during the last minute to melt.
4. **Serve**: Serve on buns topped with sauerkraut and Thousand Island dressing.

**Bacon Cheddar Ranch Burger**

**Ingredients:**

- 1 lb ground beef
- 1/2 cup cheddar cheese, shredded
- 1/4 cup ranch dressing
- 4 slices bacon, cooked and crumbled
- 4 hamburger buns
- Lettuce and tomato for topping

**Instructions:**

1. **Mix Ingredients**: In a bowl, combine ground beef, cheddar cheese, ranch dressing, and crumbled bacon. Form into four patties.
2. **Preheat Grill**: Heat grill to medium-high.
3. **Cook Patties**: Grill for about 4-5 minutes on each side until desired doneness.
4. **Serve**: Serve on buns topped with lettuce and tomato.

**Spicy Mediterranean Turkey Burger**

**Ingredients:**

- 1 lb ground turkey
- 1/4 cup feta cheese, crumbled
- 1/4 cup Kalamata olives, chopped
- 1 tablespoon red onion, finely chopped
- 1 teaspoon garlic powder
- 1 teaspoon oregano
- 4 hamburger buns
- Lettuce and tzatziki sauce for topping

**Instructions:**

1. **Mix Ingredients**: In a bowl, combine ground turkey, feta cheese, olives, red onion, garlic powder, and oregano. Form into four patties.
2. **Preheat Grill**: Heat grill to medium-high.
3. **Cook Patties**: Grill for about 5-6 minutes on each side until cooked through.
4. **Serve**: Serve on buns topped with lettuce and tzatziki sauce.

## Chipotle Turkey Burger with Avocado

**Ingredients:**

- 1 lb ground turkey
- 1 tablespoon chipotle sauce
- 1/2 teaspoon cumin
- Salt and pepper to taste
- 4 slices avocado
- 4 hamburger buns
- Cilantro for topping

**Instructions:**

1. **Mix Ingredients**: In a bowl, combine ground turkey, chipotle sauce, cumin, salt, and pepper. Form into four patties.
2. **Preheat Grill**: Heat grill to medium-high.
3. **Cook Patties**: Grill for about 5-6 minutes on each side until cooked through.
4. **Serve**: Serve on buns topped with avocado slices and cilantro.

**Maple Glazed Burger with Bacon**

**Ingredients:**

- 1 lb ground beef
- 1/4 cup maple syrup
- 4 slices bacon, cooked
- 4 hamburger buns
- Lettuce and tomato for topping

**Instructions:**

1. **Mix Ingredients**: In a bowl, combine ground beef and maple syrup. Form into four patties.
2. **Preheat Grill**: Heat grill to medium-high.
3. **Cook Patties**: Grill for about 4-5 minutes on each side until desired doneness.
4. **Serve**: Serve on buns topped with bacon, lettuce, and tomato.

## Pimento Cheese Burger

**Ingredients:**

- 1 lb ground beef
- 1/2 cup pimento cheese
- 4 hamburger buns
- Pickles for topping

**Instructions:**

1. **Preheat Grill**: Heat grill to medium-high.
2. **Form Patties**: Divide ground beef into four patties.
3. **Cook Patties**: Grill for about 4-5 minutes on each side. Add a dollop of pimento cheese during the last minute to melt.
4. **Serve**: Serve on buns topped with pickles.

**BBQ Brisket Burger**

**Ingredients:**

- 1 lb ground beef
- 1/2 cup cooked brisket, chopped
- 1/4 cup BBQ sauce
- 4 hamburger buns
- Coleslaw for topping

**Instructions:**

1. **Mix Ingredients**: In a bowl, combine ground beef, chopped brisket, and BBQ sauce. Form into four patties.
2. **Preheat Grill**: Heat grill to medium-high.
3. **Cook Patties**: Grill for about 4-5 minutes on each side until desired doneness.
4. **Serve**: Serve on buns topped with coleslaw.

## Cucumber Dill Burger

**Ingredients:**

- 1 lb ground turkey or chicken
- 1/4 cup cucumber, finely chopped
- 2 tablespoons fresh dill, chopped
- 1/4 cup Greek yogurt
- 4 hamburger buns
- Lettuce for topping

**Instructions:**

1. **Mix Ingredients**: In a bowl, combine ground turkey, cucumber, dill, and yogurt. Form into four patties.
2. **Preheat Grill**: Heat grill to medium-high.
3. **Cook Patties**: Grill for about 5-6 minutes on each side until cooked through.
4. **Serve**: Serve on buns topped with lettuce.

## Sweet Potato Black Bean Burger

**Ingredients:**

- 1 cup cooked sweet potato, mashed
- 1 can black beans, drained and rinsed
- 1/2 cup breadcrumbs
- 1 teaspoon cumin
- 1/2 teaspoon chili powder
- 4 hamburger buns
- Avocado and salsa for topping

**Instructions:**

1. **Mix Ingredients**: In a bowl, mash black beans and combine with sweet potato, breadcrumbs, cumin, and chili powder. Form into four patties.
2. **Preheat Grill**: Heat grill to medium-high.
3. **Cook Patties**: Grill for about 4-5 minutes on each side until heated through.
4. **Serve**: Serve on buns topped with avocado and salsa.

## Huli Huli Chicken Burger

**Ingredients:**

- 1 lb ground chicken
- 1/4 cup soy sauce
- 1/4 cup pineapple juice
- 1 tablespoon brown sugar
- 4 hamburger buns
- Pineapple rings for topping

**Instructions:**

1. **Mix Ingredients**: In a bowl, combine ground chicken, soy sauce, pineapple juice, and brown sugar. Form into four patties.
2. **Preheat Grill**: Heat grill to medium-high.
3. **Cook Patties**: Grill for about 5-6 minutes on each side until cooked through.
4. **Serve**: Serve on buns topped with grilled pineapple rings.

## Bourbon BBQ Burger

**Ingredients:**

- 1 lb ground beef
- 1/4 cup bourbon
- 1/4 cup BBQ sauce
- 4 hamburger buns
- Onion rings for topping

**Instructions:**

1. **Mix Ingredients**: In a bowl, combine ground beef, bourbon, and BBQ sauce. Form into four patties.
2. **Preheat Grill**: Heat grill to medium-high.
3. **Cook Patties**: Grill for about 4-5 minutes on each side until desired doneness.
4. **Serve**: Serve on buns topped with onion rings.

**Garlic Parmesan Burger**

**Ingredients:**

- 1 lb ground beef
- 2 tablespoons garlic, minced
- 1/4 cup grated Parmesan cheese
- 4 hamburger buns
- Fresh parsley for garnish

**Instructions:**

1. **Mix Ingredients**: In a bowl, combine ground beef, minced garlic, and Parmesan cheese. Form into four patties.
2. **Preheat Grill**: Heat grill to medium-high.
3. **Cook Patties**: Grill for about 4-5 minutes on each side until cooked through.
4. **Serve**: Serve on buns garnished with fresh parsley.

**Curry Chickpea Burger**

**Ingredients:**

- 1 can chickpeas, drained and rinsed
- 1/4 cup breadcrumbs
- 1 tablespoon curry powder
- 1/4 cup diced onion
- 4 hamburger buns
- Lettuce and cucumber for topping

**Instructions:**

1. **Mash Chickpeas**: In a bowl, mash chickpeas with a fork.
2. **Combine Ingredients**: Add breadcrumbs, curry powder, and diced onion. Form into four patties.
3. **Preheat Grill**: Heat grill to medium-high.
4. **Cook Patties**: Grill for about 4-5 minutes on each side until heated through.
5. **Serve**: Serve on buns topped with lettuce and cucumber.

## Apple and Gouda Burger

**Ingredients:**

- 1 lb ground beef
- 1/2 cup apple, grated
- 1/4 cup Gouda cheese, shredded
- 4 hamburger buns
- Arugula for topping

**Instructions:**

1. **Mix Ingredients**: In a bowl, combine ground beef, grated apple, and Gouda cheese. Form into four patties.
2. **Preheat Grill**: Heat grill to medium-high.
3. **Cook Patties**: Grill for about 4-5 minutes on each side until desired doneness.
4. **Serve**: Serve on buns topped with arugula.

**Dill Pickle Chicken Burger**

**Ingredients:**

- 1 lb ground chicken
- 1/4 cup dill pickles, chopped
- 1 tablespoon Dijon mustard
- 4 hamburger buns
- Lettuce for topping

**Instructions:**

1. **Mix Ingredients**: In a bowl, combine ground chicken, chopped dill pickles, and Dijon mustard. Form into four patties.
2. **Preheat Grill**: Heat grill to medium-high.
3. **Cook Patties**: Grill for about 5-6 minutes on each side until cooked through.
4. **Serve**: Serve on buns topped with lettuce.

## Steakhouse Burger with Caramelized Onions

**Ingredients:**

- 1 lb ground beef
- 1 onion, sliced
- 2 tablespoons butter
- 4 hamburger buns
- Blue cheese for topping

**Instructions:**

1. **Caramelize Onions**: In a skillet, melt butter and cook onions until golden brown.
2. **Mix Ingredients**: In a bowl, season ground beef with salt and pepper. Form into four patties.
3. **Preheat Grill**: Heat grill to medium-high.
4. **Cook Patties**: Grill for about 4-5 minutes on each side until desired doneness.
5. **Serve**: Serve on buns topped with caramelized onions and blue cheese.

## Lobster Roll Burger

**Ingredients:**

- 1 lb lobster meat, cooked and chopped
- 1/4 cup mayonnaise
- 1 tablespoon lemon juice
- 4 hamburger buns
- Butter for toasting buns

**Instructions:**

1. **Prepare Lobster**: In a bowl, combine chopped lobster meat, mayonnaise, and lemon juice.
2. **Preheat Grill**: Heat grill to medium-high.
3. **Toast Buns**: Butter buns and toast them on the grill until golden brown.
4. **Serve**: Fill buns with lobster mixture.

**Fig and Bacon Burger**

**Ingredients:**

- 1 lb ground beef
- 1/2 cup figs, chopped
- 4 slices bacon, cooked and crumbled
- 4 hamburger buns
- Goat cheese for topping

**Instructions:**

1. **Mix Ingredients**: In a bowl, combine ground beef, chopped figs, and crumbled bacon. Form into four patties.
2. **Preheat Grill**: Heat grill to medium-high.
3. **Cook Patties**: Grill for about 4-5 minutes on each side until desired doneness.
4. **Serve**: Serve on buns topped with goat cheese.

www.ingramcontent.com/pod-product-compliance
Lightning Source LLC
LaVergne TN
LVHW081500060526
838201LV00056BA/2847